Accessories ... a Girl's Best Friend

Accessories are a fashion statement. Since you have to wear shoes, make them exquisite. The gloves that warm your hands and your purse should match your outfit.

You can't be expected to go anywhere without the essentials, and no lady would leave the house without her hat!

Top off your presentation with fine jewelry and perfume, and you are ready to present yourself to the world.

patterns on pages 18 - 21

WOOL For Stitcheries

Purchase wool at your local quilt shop or fabric store. Or you can visit a resale store to purchase red and purple wool skirts or jackets. Skirts yield the most useable wool.

FELTING:

After purchasing new wool fabric or an old skirt, the wool needs to be 'felted'. 'Felting' is washing the wool in HOT water with a little detergent and a COLD rinse. Then dry the wool in a HOT dryer.

Garments can either be ripped apart before or after felting. If a garment is clean, take it apart before felting because it is easier.

Note: Any wool that has been hand-dyed has already been 'felted'.

Red Hat Shirt

Casual clothes don't have to be boring. Get the attention you deserve when you wear this bright ensemble. Decorate your favorite shirt with colorful wool appliques. With wool applique, you never need to turn the edges under... simply cut and stitch.

Stand out in a crowd with this fun shirt. Wear a red hat applique over your heart. Display your accessory pins on the other side.

see patterns on pages 22 - 23

Shoppers' Paradise Mall

Celebrate the veteran shopper and show off your embroidery skills when you stitch these adorable pillow tops or wall-hangings

These delightful projects are small enough to complete in a couple afternoons, so you will have time to make several for all your friends.

Add simple embellishments for fluff and jewelry.

see patterns on pages 24 - 27

Basic Food • Tag Sales

If you can't resist a sale, build up some energy with a chocolate coffee break. Stitch these wonderful designs.
see patterns on pages 28 - 31

Fashion Quilt

Stylish from head to toe, this quilt exhibits fashion essentials.
see patterns on pages 32 - 36

Fabulous

Women have discovered that they can look and feel fabulous at any age. It is all in the way you perceive yourself. Make one of these clever designs for the woman who has finally "come of age".

see pattern on page 46

Sensational

Do you know a sensational woman in her fifties? Recognize her "arrival" with the perfect birthday present. Celebrate her life with this amusing design. And while you're at it, make one for yourself. You'll get there before you know it!

see pattern on page 47

Sophisticated Lady

Polished and polite, the sophisticated lady turns up for every occasion with proper attire - matching hat, purse and shoes. She could easily teach Emily Post a thing or two about propriety.

see pattern on pages 48 - 49

Red Hat Lady

Delicate netting covers the eyes of this refined Lady. Tiny red seed beads adorn her ears and the rose on her lapel. A small purple ribbon and feather accent her bright red hat. Perhaps this lady is not as demure as she looks.

see pattern on page 45

spiRited • excEssive • raDiant

Truer words have n'er been stitched! This little wall hanging goes together really fast. Now you will be able to keep the Red Hat creed clearly visible at all times.

see patterns on pages 50 - 51

Red and Purple Favorites

These fabulous pincushions keep your needles nearby while you stitch wonderful projects. Express your Hat-itude with these fun-filled projects. The Spirit Bag makes a great gift. Since you will need your fancy glasses every day, make a whimsical case that expresses Red Hat creativity and don't forget to decorate your table with a classy Red Hat Welcome penny rug.

see patterns on pages 38 - 43

Sweat Suit

Casual, comfortable, and so dramatic, this ensemble will have you looking for fun places to go.

There is nothing like a new outfit to spice up your mood.

Have fun adding this colorful pantsuit to your wardrobe.

see patterns on page 37

Hot Mama Slippers • Red Boa Totebag

These slippers will keep your toes toasty warm and your attitude "Red Hat"! Have fun beading while you remember the Roaring 20's with these Cash Stash sequined purses, or make a more daring statement with a feather boa handbag.

see patterns on page 37 - 38

Ladies in Waiting

Little Red Sisterhood

Sisterhood

The Red Hat sisterhood has a great sense of humor. Capture the sense of humor with these wall hangings.

see patterns on pages 52 - 55

Collect & Decorate

Add to your frequent shopper miles when you purchase all those beads, thread and notions for your projects. Remember, basic is boring, be daring and decorate.

see patterns on pages 56 - 59

Accessories Quilt

This quilt is so much fun!

Executed in brilliant reds and purple, the border makes the perfect frame to showcase the playful appliques. Use wool for easy applique shoes, hats and purses on this colorful cotton quilt. With wool applique, you never need to turn the edges under... simply cut and stitch.

Each block offers a unique texture. Ribbons, sequins and beads give this happy creation lots of pizazz.

see patterns on pages 60 - 63

WOOL For Stitcheries

Purchase wool at your local quilt shop or fabric store. Or you can visit a resale store to purchase red and purple wool skirts or jackets. Skirts yield the most useable wool.

FELTING:

After purchasing new wool fabric or an old skirt, the wool needs to be 'felted'. 'Felting' is washing the wool in HOT water with a little detergent and a COLD rinse. Then dry the wool in a HOT dryer.

Garments can either be ripped apart before or after felting. If a garment is clean take it apart before felting because it is easier.

Note: Any wool that has been hand-dyed has already been 'felted'.

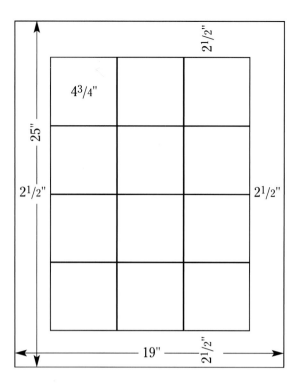

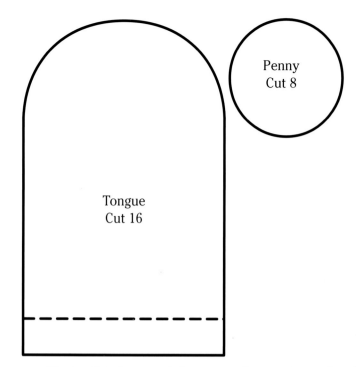

Penny
Cut 8

Tongue
Cut 16

Accessories... a Girl's Best Friend

by Betsy Chutchian

FINISHED SIZE: 19" X 29"

MATERIALS:
1 yard of dark Purple felted wool
12" x 14" Red felted wool
Scraps of medium shade purple felted wool
1 yard of brushed cotton for backing
Chenille needle DMC size 18
Embroidery needles Size 7
DMC floss: Red #321, 304; Purple #333, 3837
DMC perle cotton size 3 or 5: Red #321
DMC perle cotton size 8: Red #321, 304
Buttons:
    Eight 5/8" - 3/4"" Red buttons
    Eight 1/2" Purple buttons
    Two 3/8" Red buttons
    Six 1/8" Red buttons
Embellishments:
    Red sequins
    Gold thread
    2 Pearl charms
    12" string of tiny pearls
    Red seed beads
    Red E-beads
    2 decorative buttons
    1/4" Purple satin ribbon

INSTRUCTIONS:
All seam allowances are 1/4".
Cut a 19" x 25" piece from dark Purple wool. Mark a border 2 1/2" wide on all sides with a chalk pencil or chaco-liner. Mark a 3 across by 4 down grid within the border (4 3/4" squares).

Blanket Stitch around the outer edges with size 3 or 5 Red #321 perle cotton. Sew a Running Stitch with the same size perle cotton along the border and grid lines.

Cut out design templates for each square, some from wool, others embroidered. Follow the photo on page 3 for placement and embellishments. Applique wool shapes with 2 strands of floss or perle cotton size 8 in a Buttonhole Stitch or Whip Stitch. Stitch embroidered squares with 2 strands of floss or size 8 perle cotton.

Embellish each design with beads, embroidery, etc.

Stitch the words around border using a Stem Stitch, Backstitch or Straight Stitch with size 8 perle cotton.

Sew on buttons.

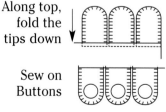

Cut out 16 Purple wool tongues. Blanket Stitch around each, using size 3 or 5 Red perle cotton. Cut out 8 Red wool 1 1/4" pennies. Attach each penny to 8 of the tongues with a Blanket Stitch in 2 strands of Purple floss. Sew a Purple button in the center of each penny with Red perle cotton.

Evenly space 8 tongues with pennies along the bottom edge of the sampler. Place the top of each tongue 1/2" under the sampler. Whip Stitch each tongue to the back with matching thread.

Along top, fold the tips down

Sew on Buttons

Evenly space 8 tongues along the top edge of the sampler. Stitch each to the back. Fold the tips of the tongues down over the top edge of the top border. Stitch the tongues in place by attaching Red buttons with Purple floss. The folded over edge creates a pocket for a decorative hanging rod.

Trim brushed cotton (backing) 1/2" larger than the sampler rectangle on all edges. Smooth backing along the back of the sampler, pinning in place. Fold edges under and stitch to back with matching thread.

Hang with a decorative rod and enjoy!

Accessories... a Girl's Best Friend

see photo on page 3

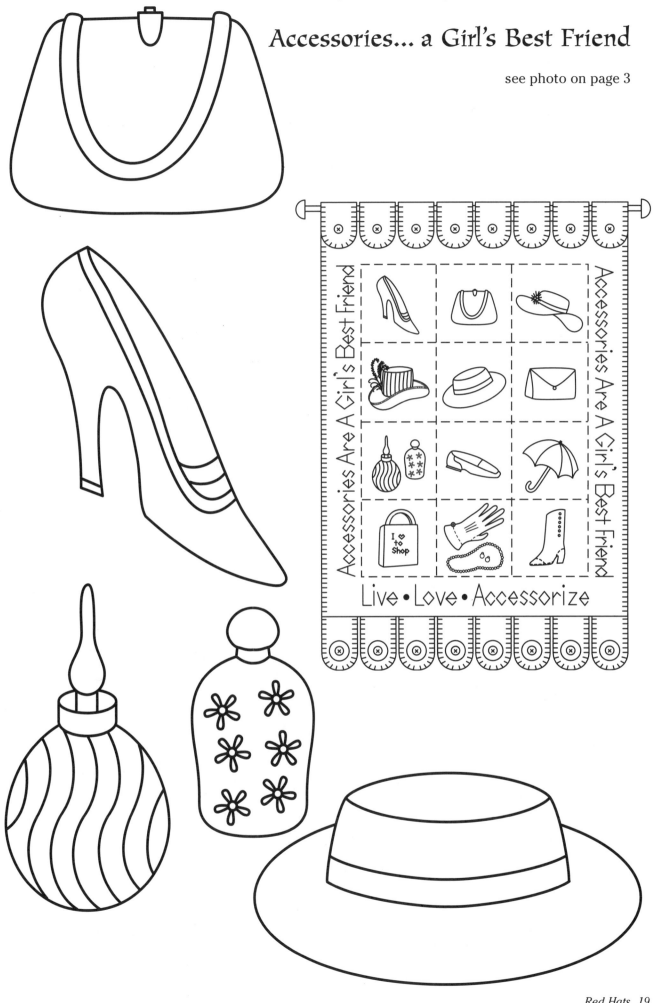

Accessories Are A Girl's Best Friend

Accessories Are A Girl's Best Friend

I ♥ to Shop

Live • Love • Accessorize

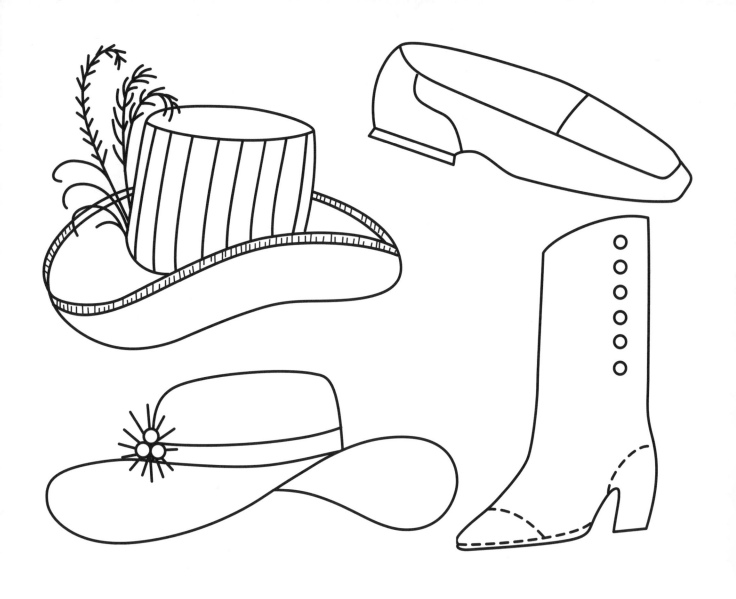

Accessories Are a Girl's

Live • Love •

Glove has a small string of pearls and pearl earrings in the block.

I ♡ to Shop

Best Friend
Accessorize

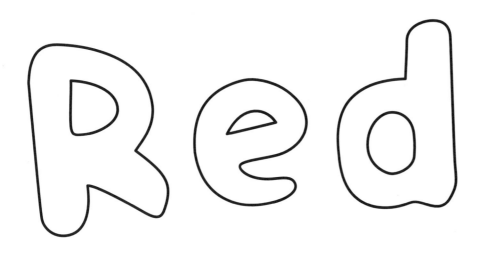

Red

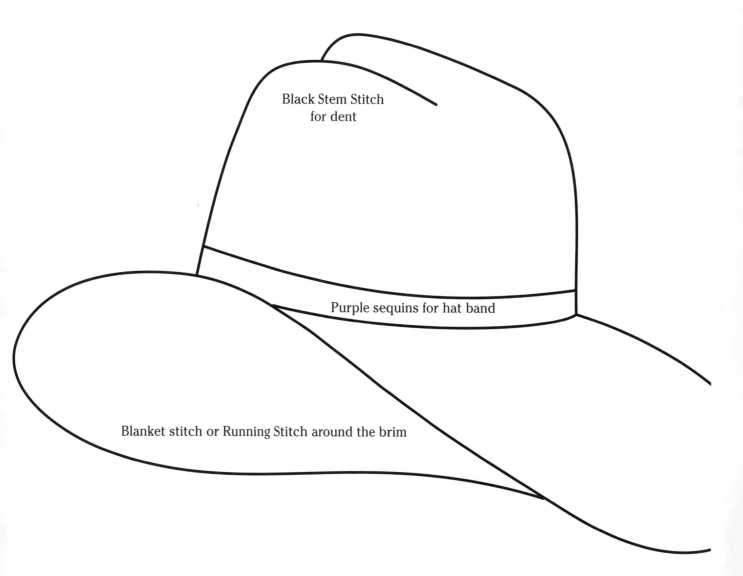

Black Stem Stitch
for dent

Purple sequins for hat band

Blanket stitch or Running Stitch around the brim

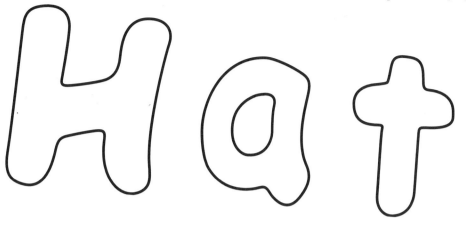

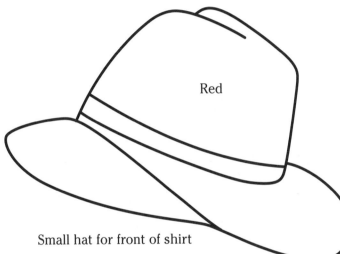

Red

Small hat for front of shirt

by Betty Edgell

MATERIALS:
One purchased shirt
12" x 15" piece of Red felted wool
Purple buttons
DMC perle cotton size 8: Red #321
1/2 yard of Purple sequin trim or
    loose sequins and seed beads

INSTRUCTIONS:
Remove buttons from a shirt and replace them with assorted Red buttons.

Using a Fly Stitch, embroider around the collar and down both sides of the front and pocket.

Applique a small hat to the front of shirt and embellish it with sequins, ribbon, etc.

Applique 'Red Hat' letters to the yoke of shirt back with a Blanket Stitch.

Using a Whip Stitch or a Blanket Stitch, applique a large Red Hat to the back of shirt below the yoke. Add a Blanket Stitch around the brim of hat.

Embellish the hat band with sequins, ribbons, buttons, braid or feathers.

Fly Stitch

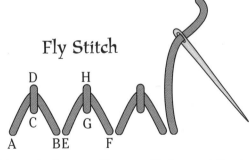

Up at A, down at B, up at C, down at D, etc.

arrival... Shopper's Paradise Mall

see photo on page 5

by Judith Lester

FINISHED SIZE: 17" x 20"

MATERIALS:
1/3 yard of muslin
1/4 yard of Purple inside border fabric
1/4 yard of Red outside border fabric
1/4 yard of Purple binding fabric
Cotton quilt batting
DMC floss: Red #321
Embellishments

INSTRUCTIONS:
See detailed instructions on page 44
CUT CENTER PIECE:
Cut the finished piece to 11" x 14".
INSIDE BORDER - Purple:
Cut 2 strips 1 1/2" x 14". Stitch to the top & bottom of piece. Cut 2 strips 1 1/2" x 13 1/2". Stitch to the sides.
OUTSIDE BORDER - Red:
Cut 2 strips 2 1/2" x 13". Stitch to the sides of piece. Cut 2 strips 2 1/2" x 20" Stitch to top and bottom.
FINISH:
Layer fabric, quilt as desired and add Purple binding.

by Judith Lester

FINISHED SIZE: 17" x 20"

MATERIALS:
1/3 yard of muslin
1/4 yard of Purple inside border fabric
1/4 yard of Red outside border fabric
1/4 yard of Purple binding fabric
Cotton quilt batting
DMC floss: Red #321
Embellishments

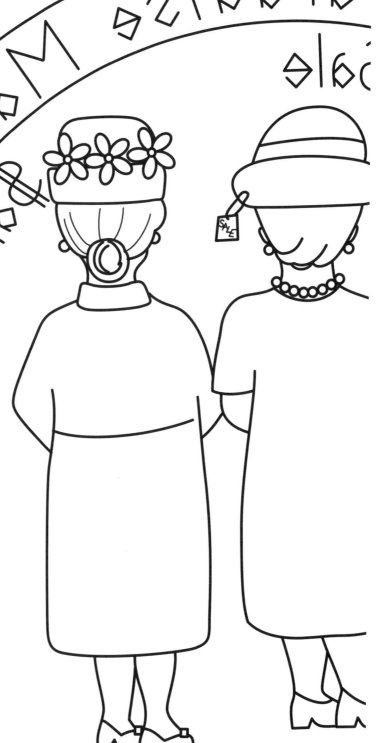

INSTRUCTIONS:
    See detailed instructions on page 44
CUT CENTER PIECE:
    Cut the finished piece to 11" x 14".
INSIDE BORDER - Purple:
    Cut 2 strips 1 1/2" x 14". Stitch to the top & bottom of piece. Cut 2 strips 1 1/2" x 13 1/2". Stitch to the sides.
OUTSIDE BORDER - Red:
    Cut 2 strips 2 1/2" x 13". Stitch to the sides of piece. Cut 2 strips 2 1/2" x 20" Stitch to top and bottom.
FINISH:
Layer fabric, quilt as desired and add Purple binding.

by Judith Lester

FINISHED SIZE: 16" x 19"

MATERIALS:

1/3 yard of muslin
1/4 yard of Purple outside border fabric
1/4 yard of Red binding fabric
Cotton quilt batting
DMC floss: Red #321, Dark Brown, Tan
Embellishments

Chocolate Chips: French Knots

Cookies: Satin Stitch Dark Brown

Flowers on Shirt: Embellish with Lazy Daisy Stitch embroidered flowers or place sequins with seed beads

chocolate

coffee

INSTRUCTIONS:
See detailed instructions on page 44

CUT CENTER PIECE:
Cut the finished piece to 11" x 14".
OUTSIDE BORDER - Purple:
Cut 2 strips 3" x 14". Stitch to the sides of piece. Cut 2 strips 3" x 16" Stitch to top and bottom.
FINISH:
Layer fabric, quilt as desired and add Red binding.

FINISHED SIZE: 17" x 21"
MATERIALS: 1/3 yard of muslin
1/4 yard of Red inside border fabric • 1/4 yard of Purple outside border fabric
1/4 yard of Red binding fabric • Cotton quilt batting
DMC floss: Red #321, Purple, Green • Embellishments

TAG SALE

10¢

50¢

So Many Tag Sales

see photo on page 6

by Judith Lester

So Many Tag Sales
So Little Time . . .

INSTRUCTIONS: *See detailed instructions on page 44*
CUT CENTER PIECE: Cut the finished piece to 12" x 16".
SIDE BORDERS:
    Cut 2 strips of Red 1 1/4" x 16". Stitch to the sides of piece.
    Cut 2 strips of Purple 2 1/2" x 16". Stitch to the sides.
TOP and BOTTOM BORDERS:
    Cut 2 strips of Red 1 1/4" x 17". Stitch to top
    and bottom of piece. Cut 2 strips of Purple
    2 1/2" x 17" Stitch to top and bottom.
FINISH:
Layer fabric, quilt as desired and add Red binding.

Fashion Quilt

by Betty Edgell

FINISHED SIZE: 28" x 37"

MATERIALS:
2/3 yard of muslin background fabric
1/4 yard of Red for inner border
2/3 yard of Purple for outer border
1/8 yard of Purple for squares
1/4 yard of Purple for binding
    (use one or 6 different coordinating Purples)
1/2 yard of Red felted wool
2 yards of cotton quilt batting
Floss:
    DMC floss Purple #550, Red #321
Embellishments:
    feathers, buttons, beads,
    scraps of silk or ribbon for hat band,
    sequins, purchased star appliques.

INSTRUCTIONS:
Use a 1/4' seam allowance throughout.
    Cut background fabric into six 12" squares.
    Choose patterns, hats, handbags and shoes. Trace patterns onto Red wool. Cut out patterns along cutting line.
    Center a motif on each background square. Applique with a Whip Stitch or a Blanket Stitch
    Embellish each design as desired. Embroider dimensional details with Purple floss.
    Cut completed squares to 10 1/2", centering each design.

SEW CORNERS TO BLOCKS:
    Cut four 3 1/2" squares from Purple fabric.
    Place one square in each corner of a block (with right sides together). Sew diagonally across each square. Flip the inside corner of each square toward the corner of the block and press.
    Repeat with all 6 blocks.

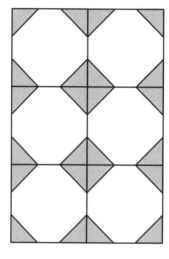 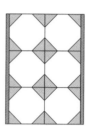 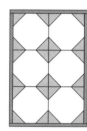  

QUILT CENTER:
    Arrange blocks and sew together.
INNER BORDER:
    Cut 2 strips 1 1/2" x 30 1/2" of Red fabric. Sew one strip to each side of the quilt center.
    Cut 2 strips 1 1/2" x 22 1/2" of Red fabric. Sew one strip to the top and one strip to the bottom of the quilt center.
OUTER BORDER:
    Cut 2 strips 3 1/4" x 32 1/2" of Purple fabric. Sew one strip to each side of the quilt center.
    Cut 2 strips 3 1/4" x 28" of Purple fabric. Sew one strip to the top and one strip to the bottom of the quilt center.

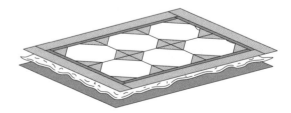

ASSEMBLE QUILT:
    Layer backing, batting, and quilt top.
BINDING:
    Cut four 2" wide x width of Purple fabric for binding.
    See binding instructions on page 33.

Pocketbook Purse :
Red felted wool.
1/2" decorative button
DMC floss Purple #550

Basic Binding Instructions

1. Cut 2" wide binding strips across the width of the fabric.
2. Sew enough strips together, end-to-end, to go around the quilt. Press seams open.
3. Fold the strip in half lengthwise, with wrong sides together.
4. Pin the raw edge of the binding strip to align with the raw edges of the top/batting/backing sandwich.
5. Machine sew binding strip in place, stitching through all layers.
6. At the corner, leave the needle in place through the fabrics and fold binding up straight. Fold it up and over into a mitered corner.
7. Fold the folded edge of the binding to the back. Whip Stitch the edge in place. Miter the corners on the front and on the back. Stitch corners closed.

Fold strip in half, wrong sides facing.

Align all raw edges.

Leave the needle in position at the corner. Fold binding up and back to miter.

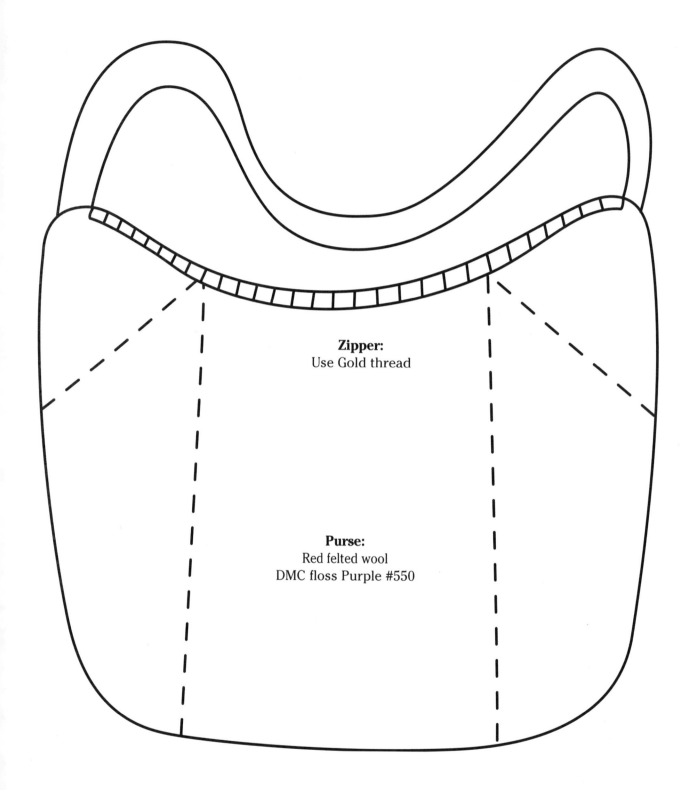

Zipper:
Use Gold thread

Purse:
Red felted wool
DMC floss Purple #550

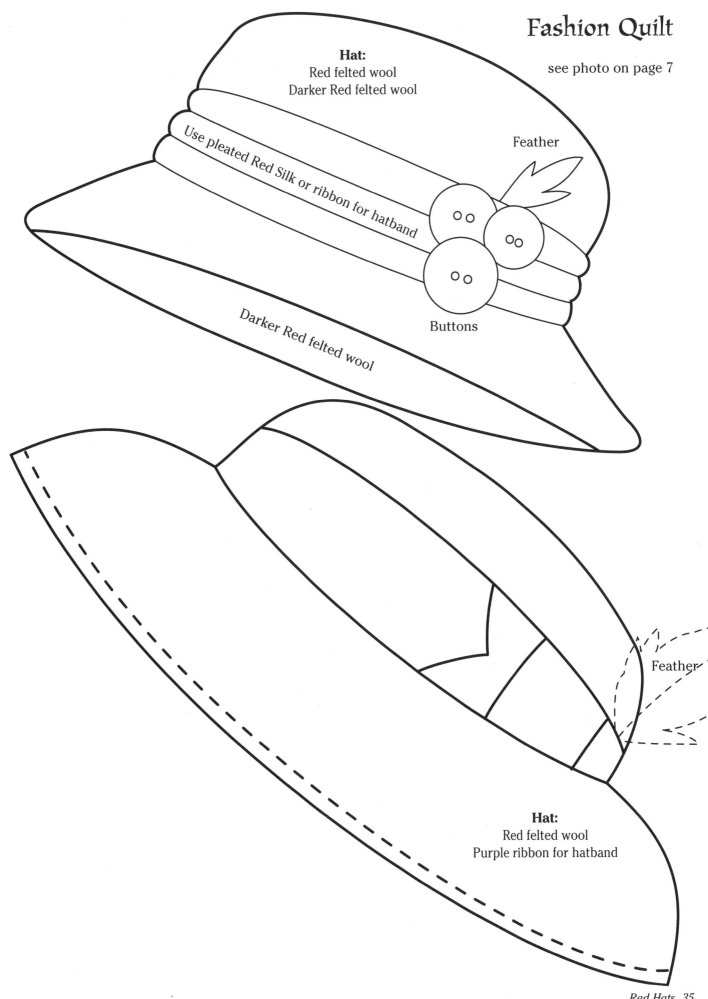

Hat:
Red felted wool
Darker Red felted wool

Feather

Use pleated Red Silk or ribbon for hatband

Buttons

Darker Red felted wool

Feather

Hat:
Red felted wool
Purple ribbon for hatband

Fashion Quilt

see photo on page 7

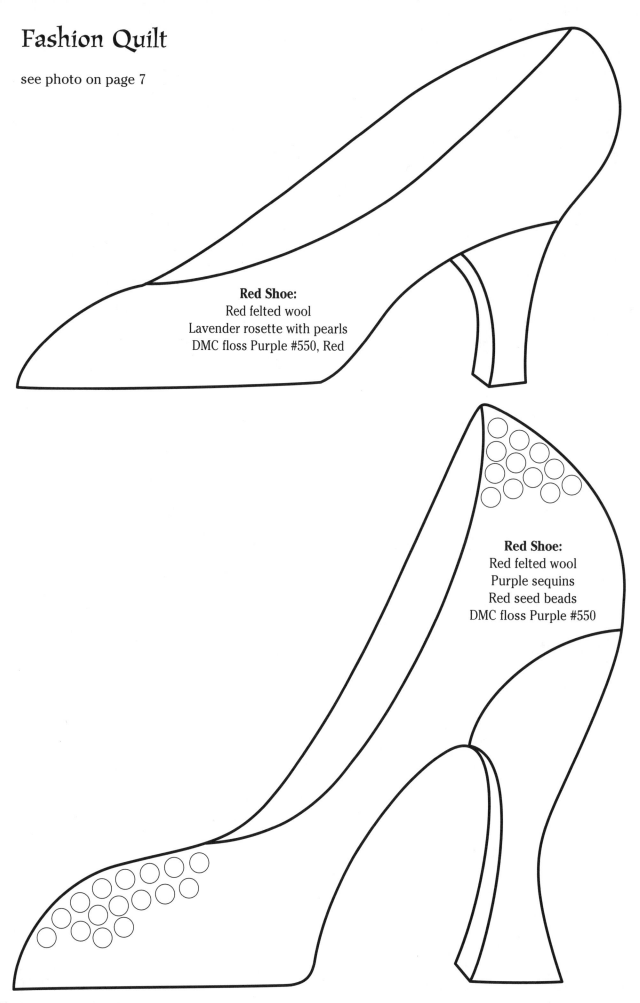

Red Shoe:
Red felted wool
Lavender rosette with pearls
DMC floss Purple #550, Red

Red Shoe:
Red felted wool
Purple sequins
Red seed beads
DMC floss Purple #550

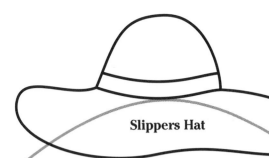

Slippers Hat

Hot Mama Slippers

see photo on page 13

by Betsy Chutchian

MATERIALS:
Purple slippers, purchased
5" square of felted Red wool
1 yard of 1/4" Purple satin ribbon
Purple and Red seed beads
DMC perle cotton size 8: Red #304
Matching thread

INSTRUCTIONS;
Blanket stitch around the edge of each slipper. Stitch only through the top edge of trim. Along the top front edge add French Knots to the open end of Blanket Stitch.

Cut a hat from Red wool, using the pattern. Position hat so the back of hat will be on the outer side of each slipper. Whip Stitch around edge of hat with Red floss. Embellish the hat with Purple ribbon for a hat band. Add beads to hat band in Running Stitch fashion, going through wool and top of slipper.

Cut a 3" piece of Purple ribbon. With matching thread, stitch a short Running Stitch along the edge and draw thread to gather ribbon into a circle. Secure the circle with a few stitches to form a flower.

Stitch a gathered flower to the back of each hat, catching the inside of loops as you stitch. Add beads to each flower center.

Sweats Outfit

see photo on page 12

by Judith Lester

MATERIALS:
One sweat shirt and matching pants
Coordinating fabric to be cut into bias strips
74 assorted Red buttons
10" x 10" piece of Red felted wool
DMC pearl cotton size 8: Red #321 • Purple #154

Pocket Pattern

INSTRUCTIONS:
Pants:
Trim off cuffs if any.
Jacket: Fold flap down.
Fold a sweat shirt in half matching the shoulders. Mark a line down the center front with a sliver of soap. Cut off the neckline and sleeve bands. Beginning at the shoulder seam, fold a gentle curve about 9" down the front to make a soft V-neck. Cut off excess at the neck.

Red Boa Bag Hat Pattern

Trim:
Use a tape measure to measure the length around the edge of neckline, down the front, around the bottom edge of sweat shirt, around the sleeve edges, and around the bottom of pants.

Cut bias strips of trim fabric 2" wide for binding. Join strips on the bias. Fold binding with wrong sides together. Press.

Place cut edges on the wrong side of sweat shirt. Stitch 1/4" from the edge. Fold binding over to the right side of sweat shirt. Use a Running Stitch and Red perle cotton to stitch the folded edge in place.

Repeat on sleeve edges and pants legs.

Cut pocket and hat from Red wool. Fold the pocket flap over pocket and pin in place. Leaving the top of pocket open, Blanket Stitch around pocket on the right side of sweat shirt using Purple perle cotton.

Applique a hat to the top left shoulder.
Add buttons to pocket and hat.

Red Boa Bag

see photo on page 13

by Betty Edgell

What a fun way to carry purchases from a shopping trip, your lunch or a small sewing project.

FINISHED SIZE: 12" x 12"
MATERIALS:
12" x 12" Purple bag
6" x 12" of Red felted wool
1 yard of Red feather boa
Crystal seed beads

INSTRUCTIONS:
Make a pattern of the hat from freezer paper. Press shiny side of freezer paper to wool with a dry iron. Using a pressing cloth, press pattern on wool. Cut out the wool hat. Pull off freezer paper.

Applique the hat on the bag. Whip Stitch the crown of hat, and Blanket Stitch the brim.

Add beads to the brim. Decorate the brim with ribbons, beads and 6" of feather boa.

Use heavy thread to attach a row of feather boa to the top of bag. Depending on the fullness of boa, you may need two layers.

Sweats Outfit Hat

× × × × × × ×

Fold flap up.

Small Purple Purse with Beaded Fringe

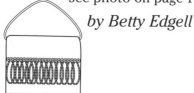

see photo on page 11

by Betty Edgell

FINISHED SIZE: 3" x 3 1/2"

MATERIALS:
5" x 8" of Purple felted wool
DMC floss: Purple #550
Red sequins and seed beads
Purple 2-cut seed beads
1/4 yard of Red RatTail cord

INSTRUCTIONS - Small Purple Purse with Beaded Fringe
Assemble Purse:
   Cut wool to 7" x 3 1/2".
   Fold each end under 1/4" and make a Running Stitch.
   Fold bottom of rectangle up 2 1/2".
   Blanket Stitch sides of purse closed.

Flap

Fold up bottom

LOOPS OF BEADED FRINGE -
Small Purple Purse with Beaded Fringe:

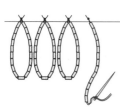

   With two strands of thread, thread beads on needle, equaling about 1 1/2", then fold and secure to the top edge of purse flap. Continue stringing beads all the way across purse edge. Secure thread.
   Stitch Red sequins and Red beads across purse flap to cover stitching. Fold flap down.
   Make a strap from 6" of Red rattail cord.

Spirit Bag

photo on page 11

by Betty Edgell

FINISHED SIZE: 7" x 12"

MATERIALS:
Two 8" x 18" pieces of felted Purple wool
Red felted wool
DMC floss: Red #321
1 1/2 yards of Red and Gold cord

INSTRUCTIONS:
   Applique a small Red hat to the center of bag. Embroider the words then add embellishments.
   Place pieces of wool together and sew on 3 sides.
   Fold the bottom corners to make triangles. Measure in 1 1/2" on each side and sew across.
   Turn bag right side out.
   Fold the top down about 2 1/2". Whip Stitch down, or leave the raw edge showing, and cut a decorative edge. Tie with a decorative cord.

Seam line

Measure in 2 1/2" on each side.
Draw a line and sew on the line.

Fold line   Fold line

Cash Stash
Small Sequin Purse

see photo on page 11

by Betty Edgell

Fill this little cash stash with money, tickets or trinkets and give as a gift, or hang as a Christmas ornament.

FINISHED SIZE: 3 1/2" x 4"

MATERIALS:
6" x 10" of Red felted wool
Purple sequins
Red seed beads
12" of Red Rattail cord
1 yard of Purple 1/8" satin ribbon

INSTRUCTIONS:
   Trace pattern on freezer paper (join 2 at the fold line). Iron patterns on wool (joining pieces 'on the fold') using a press cloth to prevent scorching. Cut around the patterns (do not cut the fold).
   Punch holes with a 1/4" hole punch beneath the scalloped edge on each end. (punch a piece of paper with the wool to get a cleaner cut.) With a pair of sharp scissors clean up any places that the hole punch missed. Machine stitch sides. Randomly stitch sequins to the front of bag. Weave a purple ribbon through the holes and tie.

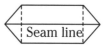

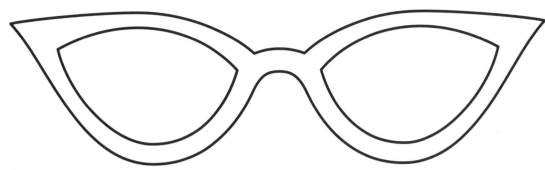

Eyeglasses Case

see photo on page 11

by Betty Edgell

FINISHED SIZE: 3¹/₂" x 6¹/₂"

MATERIALS:
8" x 11" Red felted wool
Purple sequins
Purple seed beads
8" x 11" Purple fabric for lining
DMC floss: Purple #550

INSTRUCTIONS:

Trace eyeglasses pattern on freezer paper. Cut out frames and holes. Press on one end of Red wool and trace around pattern with a White marker (a Chaco-liner works very well).

Sew sequins and beads on securely following the outline of glasses shape.

CASE:

Cut Red wool 7" x 10". With right sides of appliquéd wool and lining together, sew together on 3 sides. Fold into thirds and pin. Begin a Blanket Stitch (add a bead to each stitch) at the bottom of case. Stitch sides and around opening at top of case, leaving the top open.

Flap

Cut 1 Back
2¹/₂" x 8" including
the flap
Cut 1 Front
2¹/₂" x 4¹/₂"

Cash Stash
Red Fringed Purse

see photo on page 11

by Betty Edgell

FINISHED SIZE: 2" x 4¹/₂"

MATERIALS:
8" x 12" of Red felted wool
¹/₃ yard. of Red rat tail cord
Red seed beads
2" length of Red 3¹/₂" wide fringe
DMC floss: Purple #550
Charm or button

INSTRUCTIONS:

Cut back piece using the pattern template. Cut front piece using the pattern, with no flap.

Place the top edge of fringe along the bottom edge of right side of front, making sure that loose edges of fringe go up. When stitched and turned, fringe will hang toward the bottom. Place back and front with right sides together. Stitch around 2 sides and bottom edge.

Clip the corners. Turn purse right side out.

Blanket Stitch around the flap with Purple floss and Red beads.

Cut 12" of Rattail cord. Tie a knot in each end of the ribbon and attach to purse.

Spirit Bag

Place fringe here

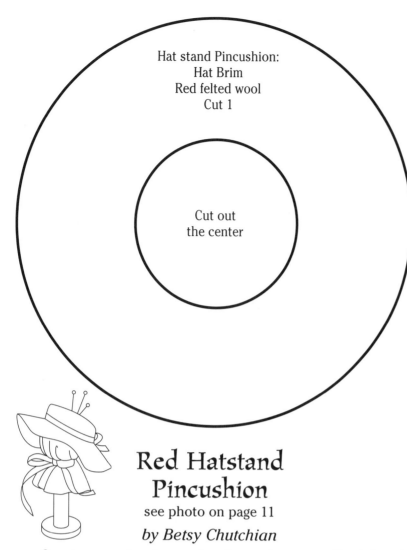

Hat stand Pincushion:
Hat Brim
Red felted wool
Cut 1

Cut out
the center

Hat stand Pincushion:
Hat Crown
Red felted wool
Cut 1

Red Hatstand Pincushion

see photo on page 11

by Betsy Chutchian

Create a centerpiece using 3 spools or candlesticks of various sizes. Embellish each hat differently.

FINISHED SIZE: 3" x 3¹/₂"

MATERIALS:
9" square of Red felted wool
7" square of White wool or flannel
Wooden spool or candlestick
Cotton, wool or fiberfill stuffing
Ribbon

INSTRUCTIONS:
Cut patterns from Red wool.

Cut a 1" x 7" Hat Strip of Red wool. Whip Stitch strip to Hat Brim, working stitched edge to the inside.

Whip Stitch Hat Crown to strip, closing strip edges with a Blanket Stitch. The stitched edges are on the inside of hat.

Embellish hat with ribbon and a bow. Make a ball of stuffing in the palm of your hand. Place it on top of the spool or candlestick.

Drape White wool or flannel over the stuffing. Tie with a ribbon.

Hat stand Pincushion:
Hat side Strip
1" x 7" Red felted wool - Cut 1

Puff Pincushion:
Side Strip
2" x 14" Purple felted wool - Cut 1

Join here

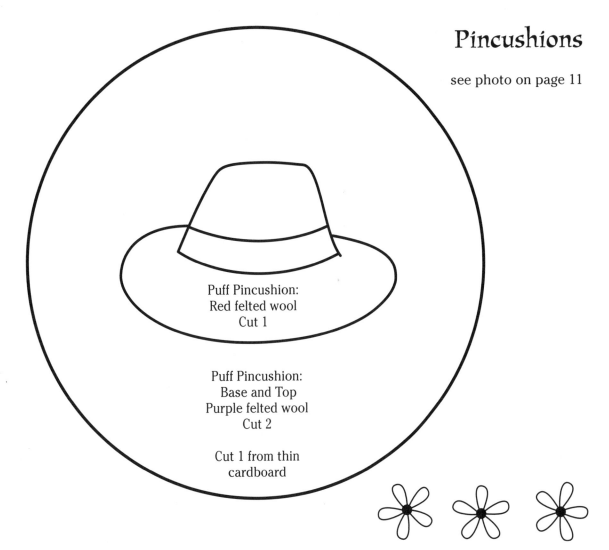

Puff Pincushion:
Red felted wool
Cut 1

Puff Pincushion:
Base and Top
Purple felted wool
Cut 2

Cut 1 from thin
cardboard

Puff Pincushion

by Betsy Chutchian

FINISHED SIZE: 5" x 5"

MATERIALS:
Purple felted wool
Red felted wool
Cotton, wool or fiberfill stuffing
DMC floss: Red #321
24" of 1/2" wide Red ribbon
Red feather

INSTRUCTIONS:
Cut 2 pieces (5" circles) from Purple felted wool. Cut a side piece 2" x 14" from Purple felted wool. Cut 1 hat from Red felted wool.

Applique hat to top of pincushion with a Blanket Stitch.

Embellish hat with 3 Lazy Daisy Stitch flowers to make a hat band. Stitch French Knots in the center of each flower.

Blanket Stitch the edges of the strip to the edges of one Purple circle (the top).

Insert the cardboard circle. Blanket Stitch the edges of to the other Purple circle (the bottom) in the same manner. Leave the side slit open.

Stuff the pincushion full then stitch the opening shut.

Tie a Red ribbon around the center of pincushion and add a small feather under the bow.

Join here

Puff Pincushion:
Side Strip
2" X 14" Purple felted wool - Cut 1

INSTRUCTIONS:

Using the pattern template, cut out hat of Red wool.

Cut oval and 16 tongues out of Purple wool.

Place the hat on oval, centering it but leaving room to embroider 'Welcome'.

Applique the hat in place with a Blanket Stitch. Draw feathers at the back of hat and embroider with a Stem Stitch.

by Betsy Chutchian

FINISHED SIZE: 15" X 20"

MATERIALS:

1/2 yard of Purple felted wool

6" x 10" of Red felted wool

DMC perle cotton size 8: Red #75

Welc

'Welcome' Penny Rug

see photo on page 11

by Betsy Chutchian

Draw or transfer 'Welcome' under the hat. Back Stitch, the word with Red perle cotton.

Embellish the hat with ribbon and embroider the feather with a Back Stitch.

Blanket Stitch around each tongue. Attach tongues to oval, placing each tongue 1/2" under the oval. Stitch in place with Purple sewing thread to match.

Blanket Stitch around the oval with Red perle cotton.

Add a backing to the penny rug with a Purple brushed cotton Purple fabric. Use the oval template adding a 1/2" seam allowance. Turn the edges under and stitch in place.

come

Tongue
Cut 16

Finishing Instructions for Small Wallhangings

MATERIALS:
1/3 yard of muslin background/backing fabric
1/4 yard of outside border fabric
1/4 yard of inside border fabric (optional)
1/4 yard of binding fabric
Thermore batting for embroidery
Cotton quilt batting
DMC floss: Red #321
Embellishments

INSTRUCTIONS:
Use a 1/4' seam allowance throughout.
Transfer pattern to a piece of muslin fabric, centering the design.

Baste cotton quilt batting to the wrong side of background fabric.

Embroider design through both layers. Stitch with 2 strands of floss using a Stem Stitch. Use one ply of floss on facial features.

Embellish with stitches, beads, buttons, sequins, trim and ribbon as desired.

CUT CENTER PIECE:
Cut the finished piece to size.

INSIDE BORDER (optional):
Cut 2 strips. Stitch to the sides of piece.
Cut 2 strips. Stitch to top and bottom.

OUTSIDE BORDER:
Cut 2 strips. Stitch to the sides of piece.
Cut 2 strips. Stitch to top and bottom.

LAYERS:
Layer backing, a second layer of cotton batting and piece. Quilt through all layers as desired.

BINDING:
Cut 2 strips 2" x width of fabric. Sew strips together end-to-end. Fold in half lengthwise and press. Position raw edges of binding even with outside edge of border. Stitch along the edge.

Turn folded edge to the back. Whip Stitch in place on the back.

see binding illustrations on page 33

'Tinting' with Crayons

Crayons Aren't Paints - Even though ironing softens the crayon, their hard nature means that some of the texture of the fabric and the strokes you make will show through - just like when you make a rubbing over a penny. Making your strokes in the same direction can be challenging in large areas, which is why projects with smaller individual areas of color are best suited to crayon tinting.

Tip: Practice on extra muslin first.

Supplies - Muslin fabric, 24 colors of crayons (or more), embroidery floss, embroidery hoop, micron pen, needle

Crayon Hints - Besides being convenient, crayons come in beautiful colors and aren't intimidating. Simply color in the spaces to create the look you want.

 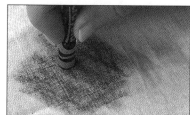

Build Up Color, Edges In

Add layers of crayon color with the strokes going in one direction, or opposite directions for a darker effect. Start lightly - you can always add more. Shading built up from the edges inward helps model or add depth to pieces, so that the tinted areas are not only colorful but three-dimensional as well. You can even choose to leave an area completely open to give a strong highlight.

Use the Correct End

For filling in color, the blunt end of the crayon works best and it works even better if the hard edge is rounded off a little before you start. Keep the pointed end for details or adding a fine shaded line to edges.

Tip: Let the Fabric Do the Work

A shaded fabric (white on white or off white) adds depth to your shading. Larger designs are a little better than fine ones because they give more variety.

1. Position fabric over a pattern, secure corners with masking tape.

Trace pattern outline directly onto muslin with a blue-line water erase pen or a pencil.

2. Place fabric on a pad of extra fabric and color areas with regular children's crayons.

Color the pattern well with crayon color.

3. Sandwich the fabric between two sheets of plain paper.

Iron on 'cotton' setting to 'set' the crayon colors.

4. If desired, back design with another piece of fabric, place fabric or layers in an embroidery hoop.

Use 3-ply floss to outline the design.

Red Hat Lady Lives Here

see photo on page 9

by Judith Lester

FINISHED SIZE: 13" x 14"

MATERIALS:
$1/3$ yard of muslin
$1/4$ yard of Red border fabric
$1/4$ yard of Red binding fabric
Cotton quilt batting
DMC floss: Red #321
Embellishments:
Feather • Red tulle netting
$1/4$ yard of $1/8$" Purple ribbon

INSTRUCTIONS:
See detailed instructions on page 44

CUT CENTER PIECE:
Cut the finished piece to $81/2$" x $91/2$".

BORDER - Red:
Cut 2 strips $21/4$" x $81/2$". Stitch to top & bottom of piece. Cut 2 strips $21/4$" x 13". Stitch to the sides.

FINISH:
Layer fabric, quilt as desired and add Red binding.

Ribbon

Feather

Tulle netting

Red Hat Lady Lives Here

Over 50 and Fabulous

see photo on page 8

by Judith Lester

FINISHED SIZE: 14" x 14"

MATERIALS:

1/3 yard of muslin
1/4 yard of Red border fabric
1/4 yard of Red binding fabric
Red felted wool for hat
Cotton quilt batting
DMC floss: Red #321
Embellishments:
1/4" wide Red satin ribbon
2 buttons
Small silk flowers
Red tulle netting

INSTRUCTIONS:
See detailed instructions on page 44

CUT CENTER PIECE:
Cut the finished piece to 10" x 10".

BORDER - Red:
Cut 2 strips 2 1/2" x 10". Stitch to the sides of piece. Cut 2 strips 2 1/2" x 14 " Stitch to top and bottom.

FINISH: Layer fabric, quilt as desired and add Red binding.

Red ribbon

Red Net:
Tuck a piece of Red tulle under the hat and stitch in place.

Small Silk flowers

Buttons

Over 50 and Fabulous

INSTRUCTIONS:

See detailed instructions on page 44

CUT CENTER PIECE:

Cut the finished piece to 10" x 10".

BORDER - Red:

Cut 4 strips 2½" x 14". Stitch one to each side of piece. Stitch one to the top and one to the bottom.

NOTE:

On this piece each corner is 'mitered' to create a 'frame' effect. Sew each strip to a side, then sew strips together at a 45 degree angle to create a 'miter' on the front side.

FINISH:

Layer fabric, quilt as desired and add Red binding.

see photo on page 8

by Judith Lester & Betty Edgell

FINISHED SIZE: 14" x 14"

MATERIALS:
1/3 yard of muslin
1/4 yard of Purple border fabric
1/4 yard of Purple binding fabric
Red felted wool for hat
Cotton quilt batting
DMC floss: Red #321
Embellishments:
Pearl button
Small silk flowers

Miter the corners for a frame.

Over 50 and Sensational

Sophisticated Lady

see photo on page 9

by Betsy Chutchian

FINISHED SIZE: 16" x 16"

MATERIALS:
1/3 yard of muslin
1/4 yard of Red border fabric
1/4 yard of Red binding fabric
Red felted wool
Purple felted wool
Cotton quilt batting
DMC floss: Red #321
Embellishments:
2 Pearls for earrings
Purple seed beads
Red seed beads
1 Red button

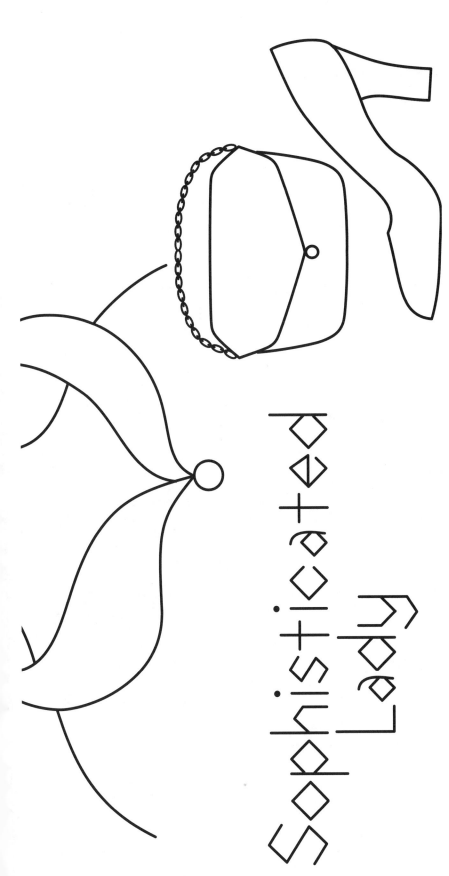

INSTRUCTIONS:
   See detailed instructions on page 44
CUT CENTER PIECE:
   Cut the finished piece to 12 1/2" x 12 1/2".
BORDER - Red:
   Cut 2 strips 2 1/4" x 12 1/2". Stitch to the sides of piece. Cut 2 strips 2 1/4" x 16". Stitch to top and bottom.
FINISH:
Layer fabric, quilt as desired and add Red binding.

by Betsy Chutchian

FINISHED SIZE: 15" x 20"

MATERIALS:

1/3 yard of muslin

1/4 yard of Purple border fabric

1/4 yard of Purple binding fabric

Red felted wool

Ten tiny Red buttons for flower centers

Cotton quilt batting

DMC floss: Red #321 and Purple #333

INSTRUCTIONS:

See detailed instructions on page 44

CUT CENTER PIECE:

Cut the finished piece to $10^{1}/_{2}$" x $15^{1}/_{2}$".

BORDER - Purple:

Cut 2 strips $2^{3}/_{4}$" x $15^{1}/_{2}$". Stitch to the sides of piece.

Cut 2 strips $2^{3}/_{4}$" x 15". Stitch to top and bottom.

FINISH:

Layer fabric, quilt as desired and add Purple binding.

spiRited

ExcEssive

raDiant

deligHtful

deligHtful

remArkable

sophisTicated

Little Red Siste

Little Red Sisterhood

see photo on page 14

by Betsy Chutchian

FINISHED SIZE: 17" x 21"

MATERIALS:
1/3 yard of muslin
1/4 yard of Purple inside border fabric
1/4 yard of Red outside border fabric
1/4 yard of Red binding fabric
Cotton quilt batting
DMC floss: Red #321,
Purple #550, Green
Embellishments

INSTRUCTIONS:
See detailed instructions on page 44

CUT CENTER PIECE:
Cut the finished piece to 10 1/2" x 15".

INSIDE BORDER - Purple:
Cut 2 strips 1 1/2" x 10 1/2". Stitch to the sides of piece. Cut 2 strips 1 1/2" x 16 1/2". Stitch to top and bottom.

OUTSIDE BORDER - Red:
Cut 2 strips 3" x 11 1/2". Stitch to the sides of piece. Cut 2 strips 3" x 21" Stitch to top and bottom.

FINISH:
Layer fabric, quilt as desired and add Red binding.

isterhood

Ladies in Wait

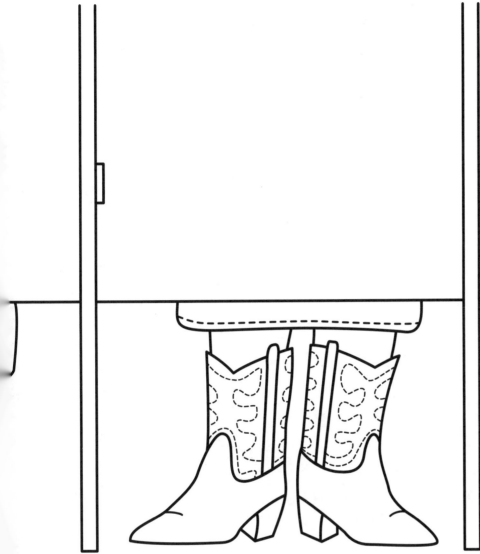

Ladies in Waiting...

see photo on page 14

by Betty Edgell

FINISHED SIZE: 16" x 20"

MATERIALS:

1/3 yard of muslin

1/4 yard of Purple inside border fabric

1/4 yard of Red outside border fabric

1/4 yard of Purple binding fabric

Cotton quilt batting

DMC floss: Red #321, Purple #550

INSTRUCTIONS:

See detailed instructions on page 44

CUT CENTER PIECE:

Cut the finished piece to 10" x 141/2".

INSIDE BORDER - Purple:

Cut 2 strips 11/2" x 10". Stitch to the sides of piece. Cut 2 strips 11/2" x 161/2". Stitch to top and bottom.

OUTSIDE BORDER - Red:

Cut 2 strips 21/2" x 121/2". Stitch to the sides of piece. Cut 2 strips 21/2" x 20" Stitch to top and bottom.

FINISH:

Layer fabric, quilt as desired and add Purple binding.

ting

*by Betsy Chutchian
and Judith Lester*

FINISHED SIZE: 16" x 21"

MATERIALS:

1/3 yard of muslin
1/4 yard of Red inside border fabric
1/4 yard of Purple outside border fabric
1/4 yard of Red binding fabric
Cotton quilt batting
DMC floss: Red #321, Purple #3837
Embellishments

STITCHING TIPS:

Facial features: 1 strand Red floss in tiny Backstitch.
Feathers, hat, hair, face, purse, belt, arms, legs:
    2 strands Red floss in Stem Stitch.
Bow, hat band, dress, shoes:
    2 strands Purple floss in Stem Stitch.
Flower: 2 strands Red floss in Lazy Daisy Stitch.
Purse handle: 2 strands Purple floss in chain stitch.
Letters: 2 strands Red floss in a Backstitch.

EMBELLISHMENT TIPS:

Necklace: 2 strands of Gold thread in French Knots
Star: 2 strands of Gold thread in Straight Stitch
Bracelet, ring, fringe: Purple seed beads
Bracelet: Red seed beads
Bangle bracelet: Red E-beads
Dress: 1/4" tiny Red buttons
Earrings and belt buckle: 2 strands Gold thread in Chain Stitch.

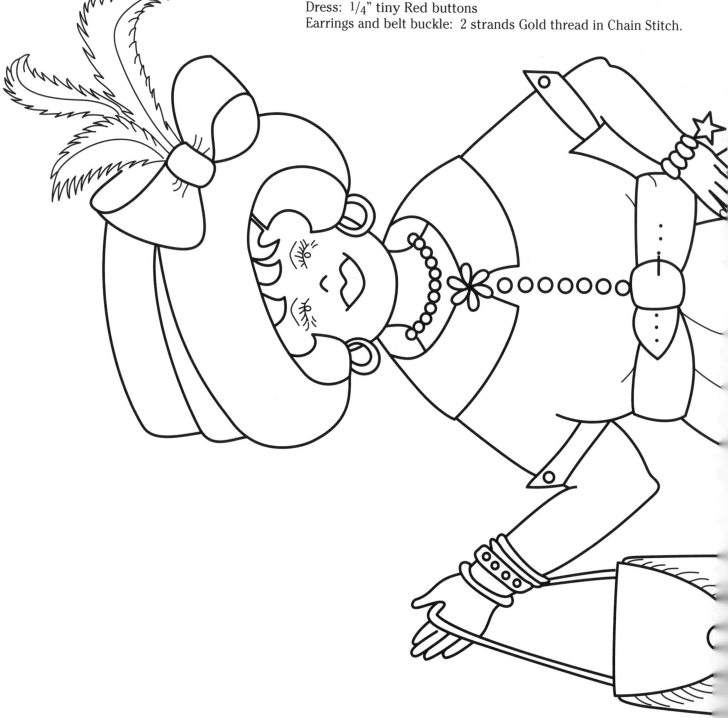

If You Can't Hide It... Decorate It!

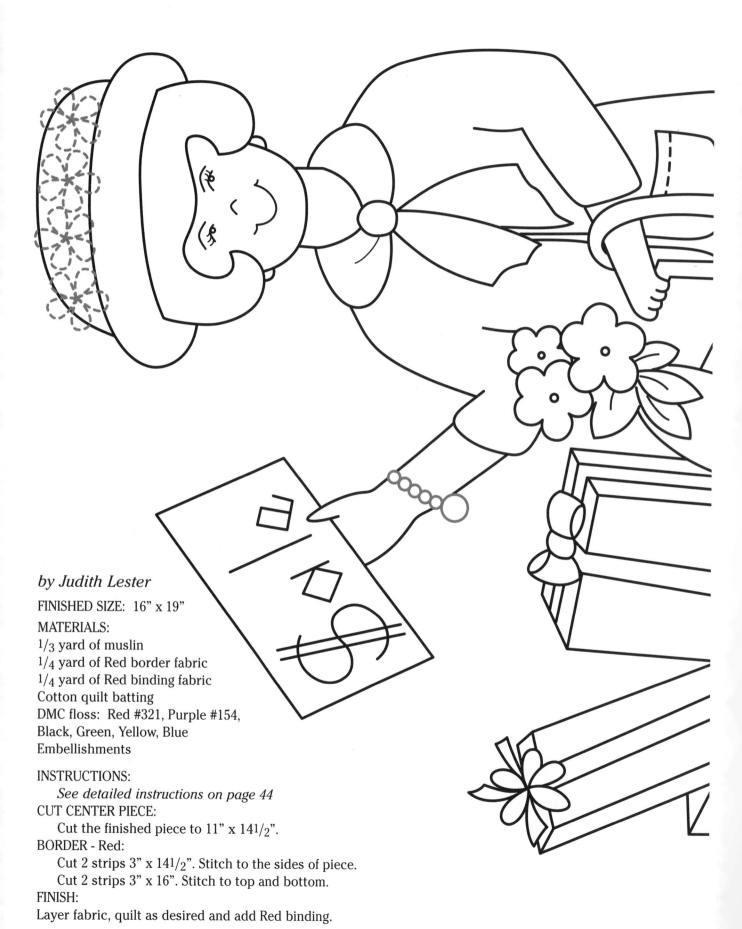

by Judith Lester

FINISHED SIZE: 16" x 19"
MATERIALS:
1/3 yard of muslin
1/4 yard of Red border fabric
1/4 yard of Red binding fabric
Cotton quilt batting
DMC floss: Red #321, Purple #154,
Black, Green, Yellow, Blue
Embellishments

INSTRUCTIONS:
    See detailed instructions on page 44
CUT CENTER PIECE:
    Cut the finished piece to 11" x 14 1/2".
BORDER - Red:
    Cut 2 strips 3" x 14 1/2". Stitch to the sides of piece.
    Cut 2 strips 3" x 16". Stitch to top and bottom.
FINISH:
Layer fabric, quilt as desired and add Red binding.

see photo on page 15

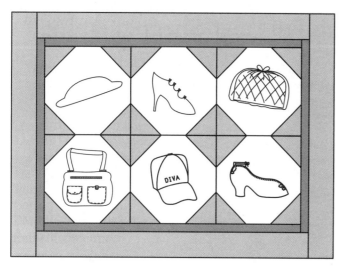

Accessories Quilt

by Judith Lester

FINISHED SIZE: 29" x 39"

MATERIALS:
2/3 yard of muslin background fabric
1/4 yard of Purple for inner border
2/3 yard of Red for outer border
1/4 yard of Red for binding
1/8 yard Red for squares
   (use one or 6 different coordinating Reds)
1/2 yard of Red felted wool
12" x 9" of Purple felted wool
2 yards of cotton quilt batting
Floss:
   DMC floss Purple #550
Embellishments:
   feathers, beads, Red tulle netting,
   scraps of silk or ribbon for hat band,
   sequins, purchased star appliques.

INSTRUCTIONS:
All seam allowances are 1/4"
   Cut background fabric into six 12" squares.
   Choose patterns, hats, handbags and shoes. Trace patterns onto Red wool. Cut out patterns along cutting line.
   Center a motif on each background square. Applique with a Whip Stitch or Blanket Stitch.
   Embellish each design as desired. Embroider dimensional details with Purple floss.
   Cut completed squares to 10 1/2", centering each design.

SEW CORNERS TO BLOCKS:
   Cut four 3 1/2" squares from Red fabric.
   Place one square in each corner of a block (with right sides together). Sew diagonally across each

square. Flip the inside corner of each square toward the corner of the block and press.
   Repeat with all 6 blocks.

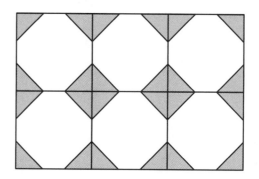

QUILT CENTER:
   Arrange blocks and sew together.

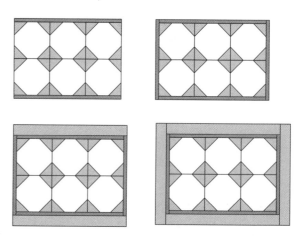

INNER BORDER:
   Cut 2 strips 1 1/2" x 30 1/2" of Purple fabric. Sew one strip to the top and one strip to the bottom of the quilt center.
   Cut 2 strips 1 1/2" x 22 1/2" of Purple fabric. Sew one strip to each side of the quilt center.
OUTER BORDER:
   Cut 2 strips 4 1/4" x 32 1/2" of Red fabric. Sew one strip to the top and one strip to the bottom of the quilt center.
   Cut 2 strips 4 1/4" x 29" of Red fabric. Sew one strip to each side of the quilt center.

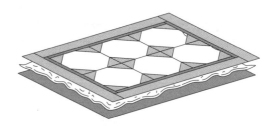

ASSEMBLE QUILT:
   Layer backing, batting, and quilt top.
BINDING:
   Cut four 2 1/2" wide x width of Red fabric for binding.
   See binding illustrations on page 33

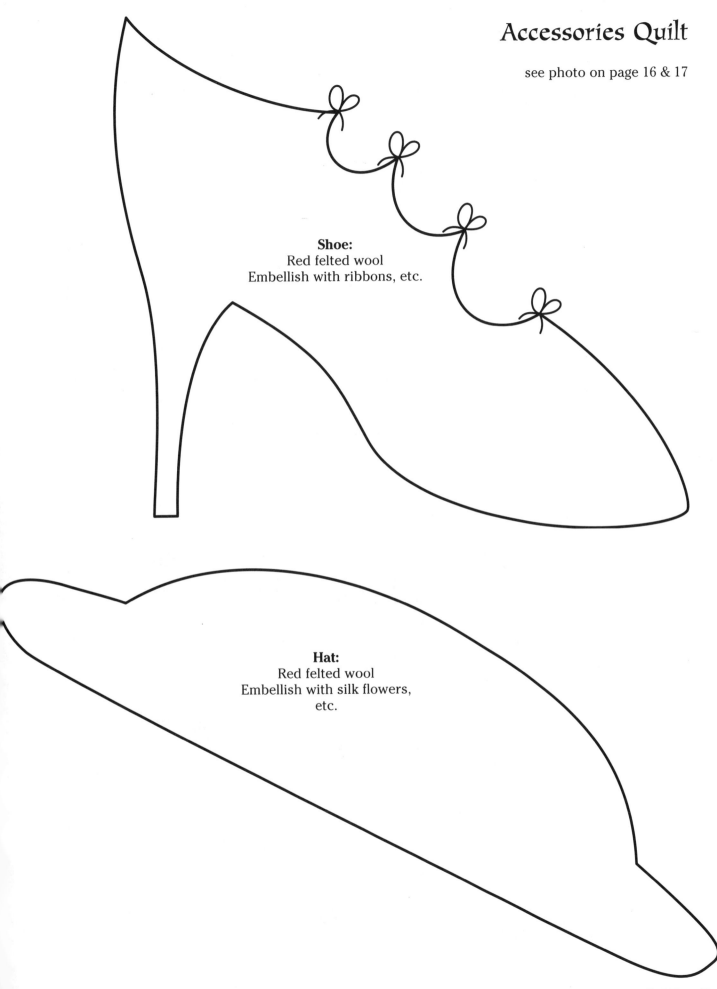

Accessories Quilt

see photo on page 16 & 17

Shoe:
Red felted wool
Embellish with ribbons, etc.

Hat:
Red felted wool
Embellish with silk flowers,
etc.

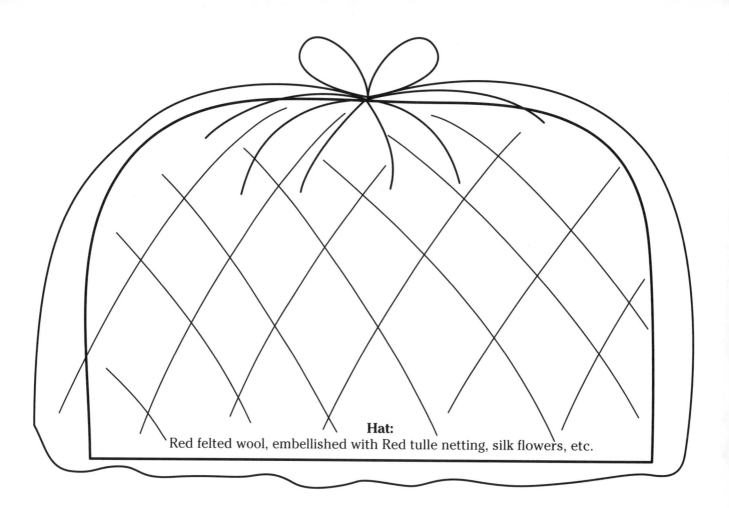

Hat:
Red felted wool, embellished with Red tulle netting, silk flowers, etc.

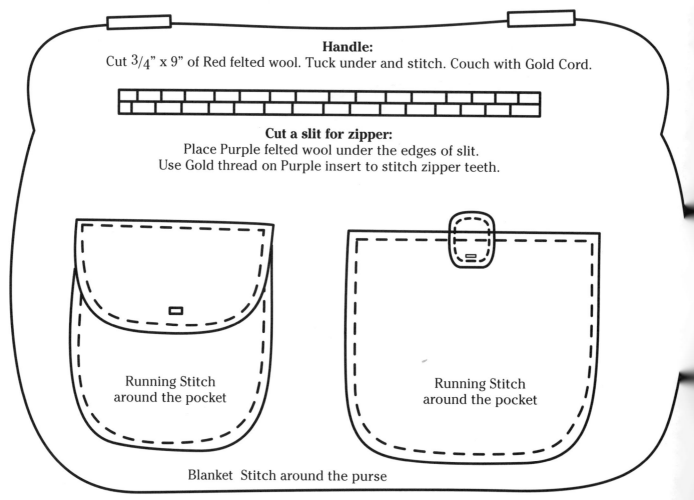

Handle:
Cut 3/4" x 9" of Red felted wool. Tuck under and stitch. Couch with Gold Cord.

Cut a slit for zipper:
Place Purple felted wool under the edges of slit.
Use Gold thread on Purple insert to stitch zipper teeth.

Running Stitch
around the pocket

Running Stitch
around the pocket

Blanket Stitch around the purse

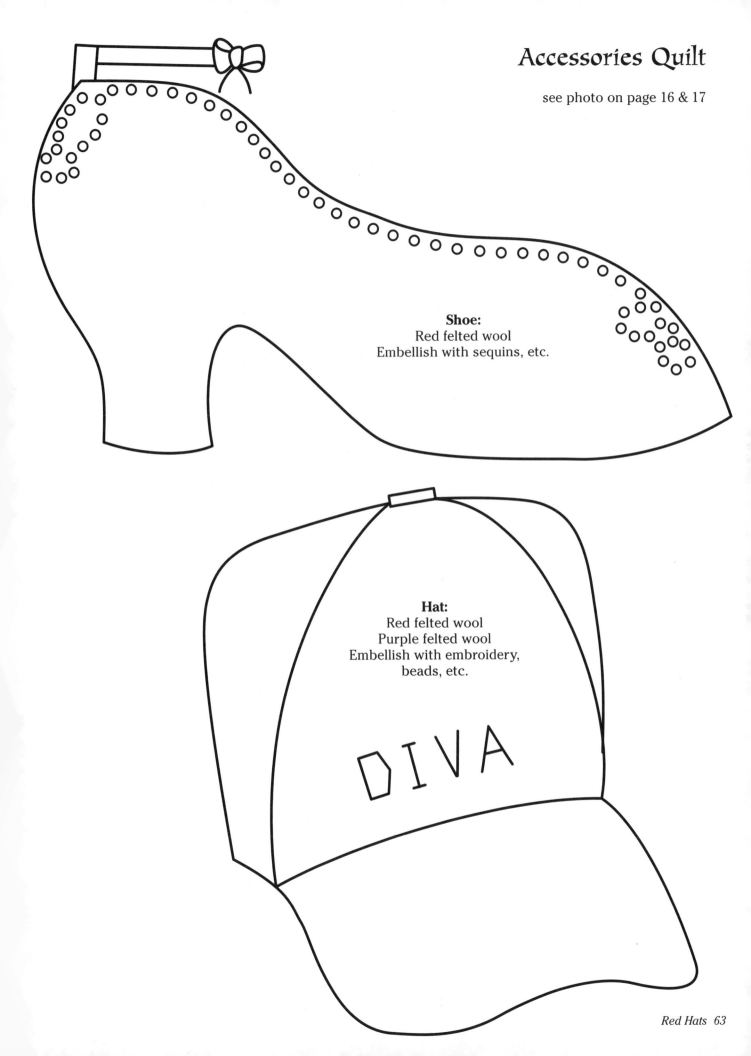

Shoe:
Red felted wool
Embellish with sequins, etc.

Hat:
Red felted wool
Purple felted wool
Embellish with embroidery,
beads, etc.

DIVA

We Love to Meet and Eat!

see photo on page 67
by Judith Lester

FINISHED SIZE: 17" x 20"

MATERIALS: 1/3 yard of muslin • 1/4 yard of Red border fabric
1/4 yard of Red binding fabric • Cotton quilt batting
DMC floss: Red #321, Purple #154, Green, Blue, Black, Yellow,
Tan, Brown • Embellishments

We Love to Meet

INSTRUCTIONS: *See detailed instructions on page 44*
CUT CENTER PIECE: Cut the finished piece to 12" x 15".
BORDER - Red: Cut 2 strips 3" x 15". Stitch to top & bottom of piece.
    Cut 2 strips 3" x 17" Stitch to the sides.
FINISH: Layer fabric, quilt as desired and add binding.

Meet and Eat!

Embroidery Stitches

Working with Floss.
Separate embroidery floss.

Use 24" lengths of floss and a #8 embroidery needle.

Use 2 to 3 ply floss to outline large elements of the design and to embroider larger and more stylized patterns.

Use 2 ply for the small details on some items.

Pay attention to backgrounds.

When working with lighter-colored fabrics, do not carry dark flosses across large unworked background areas. Stop and start again to prevent unsightly 'ghost strings' from showing through the front.

Another option is to back tinted muslin with another layer of muslin before you add embroidery stitches. This will help keep 'ghost strings' from showing.

Blanket Stitch

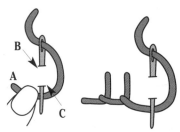

Come up at A, hold the thread down with your thumb, go down at B. Come back up at C with the needle tip over the thread. Pull the stitch into place. Repeat, outlining with the bottom legs of the stitch. Use this stitch to edge fabrics.

Chain Stitch

Come up at A. To form a loop, hold the thread down with your thumb, go down at B (as close as possible to A). Come back up at C with the needle tip over the thread. Repeat to form a chain.

Cross Stitch

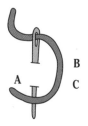

Make a diagonal Straight stitch (up at A, down at B) from upper right to lower left. Come up at C and go down at D to make another diagonal Straight stitch the same length as the first one. The stitch will form an X.

French Knot

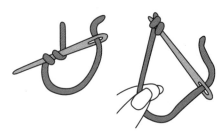

Come up at A. Wrap the floss around the needle 2 to 3 times. Insert the needle close to A. Hold the floss and pull the needle through the loops gently.

Herringbone Stitch

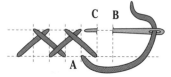

Come up at A. Make a slanted stitch to the top right, inserting the needle at B. Come up a short distance away at C.

Insert the needle at D to complete the stitch. Bring the needle back up at the next A to begin a new stitch. Repeat.

Lazy Daisy Stitch

Come up at A. Go down at B (right next to A) to form a loop. Come back up at C with the needle tip over the thread. Go down at D to make a small anchor stitch over the top of the loop.

Running Stitch

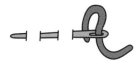

Come up at A. Weave the needle through the fabric, making short, even stitches. Use this stitch to gather fabrics, too.

Satin Stitch

Work small straight stitches close together and at the same angle to fill an area with stitches. Vary the length of the stitches as required to keep the outline of the area smooth.

Stem Stitch

Work from left to right to make regular, slanting stitches along the stitch line. Bring the needle up above the center of the last stitch. Also called 'Outline' stitch.

Straight Stitch

Come up at A and go down at B to form a simple flat stitch. Use this stitch for hair for animals and for simple petals on small flowers.

Whip Stitch

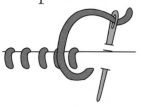

Insert the needle under a few fibers of one layer of fabric. Bring the needle up through the other layer of fabric. Use this stitch to attach the folded raw edges of fabric to the back of pieces or to attach bindings around the edges of quilts and coverlets.